Neon

and the Noble Gases

THE PERIODIC TABLE

Nigel Saunders

Design: David Poole and Tinstar Design Limited
    (www.tinstar.co.uk)
Illustrations: Geoff Ward and Paul Fellows
Picture Research: Rosie Garai
Originated by Blenheim Colour Ltd.
Printed in China by South China
    Printing Company

07 06 05 04 03
10 9 8 7 6 5 4 3 2 1

Library of Congress Cataloging-in-Publication Data
Saunders, N. (Nigel)
   Neon and the noble gases / Nigel Saunders.
      v. cm. -- (The periodic table)
Includes bibliographical references and index.
Contents: Elements and atomic structure -- The periodic table, neon and
the noble gases -- Helium -- Neon -- Argon -- Krypton -- Xenon -- Radon
-- Useful information about the noble gases.
   ISBN 1-40340-875-0 (lib. bdg.) -- ISBN 1-40343-519-7 (pbk.)
   1. Neon--Juvenile literature. 2. Gases, Rare--Juvenile literature.
[1. Neon. 2. Gases, Rare.] I. Title. II. Series.
   QD181.N5 S38 2003
   546'.75--dc21
                           2002154194

Acknowledgments
The author and publishers are grateful to the following for permission to reproduce copyright material:

p. 4 Redferns; pp. 9, 10, 17 Wally McNamee/Corbis; p. 15 Charles D Winters/Science Photo Library; pp. 18, 20 Alfred Pasieka/Science Photo Library; pp. 21, 27, 36 Charles D Winters/Science Photo Library; pp. 30, 32, 34 Graham Neden/Ecoscene/Corbis; p. 35 Bettman/Corbis; p. 37 Roger Ressmeyer/Corbis; p. 38 Ed Eckstein/Corbis; p. 39 Patimer/Kane, Inc./Corbis; p. 40 Paul A Souders/Corbis; p. 42 Roger Ressmeyer/Corbis; p. 45 Roger Ressmeyer/Corbis; p. 47 Jerry Wachter/Science Photo Library; p. 49 (top) Corbis; p. 49 (bottom) NASA; p. 50 Roger Ressmeyer/Corbis; p. 52 Science Photo Library.

Cover photograph of a neon light reproduced with permission of Getty Images.

Special thanks to Theodore Dolter for his review of this book.

Disclaimer
All the Internet addresses (URLs) given in this book were valid at the time of going to press. However, due to the dynamic nature of the Internet, some addresses may have changed, or sites may have ceased to exist since publication. While the author and publishers regret any inconvenience this may cause readers, no responsibility for any such changes can be accepted by either the author or the publishers.

Words appearing in bold, **like this,** are explained in the Glossary.

Contents

Elements and Atomic Structure

If you look around, you will see metals, plastics, water, and lots of other solids and liquids. You cannot see the gases in the air, but you know they are there, just as there are many other gases. Incredibly, over 19 million different substances have been discovered, named, and cataloged. About 4,000 substances are added to the list every day. All of these substances are made from just a few simple building blocks called **elements.**

Elements

There are about 90 naturally occurring elements and a few artificial ones. An element is a substance that cannot be broken down into simpler substances using chemical **reactions.** About three-quarters of the elements are metals, such as iron and aluminum, and most of the rest are nonmetals, such as carbon, oxygen, and neon. When elements join together in chemical reactions, they form **compounds.**

Compounds

There are countless ways in which two or more elements can join together to make compounds. Nearly all of the millions of different substances in the world are compounds. For example, aluminum oxide is made when aluminum and oxygen react together, and carbon dioxide is made when carbon and oxygen react together. Neon and the other elements in group 18 are unusual because they are very unreactive, and only react with other elements under extreme conditions, if they react at all.

Everything you can see here, including the DJ and his equipment, is made from some of the millions of substances in the world. Most are compounds, but the air is mostly a mixture of elements.

Atoms

Every substance is made up of tiny particles called **atoms.**
An element contains just one type of atom, and a compound
contains two or more types joined together. You cannot see
atoms, even with a light microscope, because they are
incredibly small. If you could line up 13 million neon atoms
side by side, the line would be only 0.039 inch (1 mm) long!

Atoms are made up of even smaller particles called **protons,
neutrons,** and **electrons.** There is a tiny **nucleus** at the
center of each atom that contains the protons and neutrons.
The electrons are arranged in different shells around the
nucleus. The number of electrons in an atom and the way they
are arranged around the nucleus determines how an element
reacts. However, most of an atom is empty space—if an atom
were blown up to be the same size as an Olympic running
track, its nucleus would be only as big as a pea!

nucleus containing
protons and neutrons

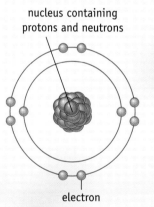

*This is a model of a
neon atom. Each element
has a different number of
protons in its nucleus.
A neon atom contains
ten protons and ten
neutrons, and it has ten
electrons arranged in two
shells around its nucleus.*

electron

Elements and groups

Different elements react with other substances in different
ways. When scientists first began to study chemical
reactions, this made it difficult for them to make sense of
the reactions they observed. In 1869, a Russian chemist
named Dimitri Mendeleev put each element into one of eight
groups in a table. Each group contained elements with
similar chemical properties. This made it much easier for
chemists to figure out what to expect when they reacted
different elements together. The modern **periodic table** is
based on the observations of Mendeleev.

The Periodic Table, Neon, and the Noble Gases

Chemists built on Mendeleev's work and eventually produced the modern **periodic table,** seen here. Each row in the table is called a **period,** and the **elements** within each period are arranged in order of increasing **atomic number** (number of **protons** in the **nucleus**). Each column in the table is called a **group.** The elements in each group have similar chemical properties. For example, the elements in group 1 are very reactive, soft metals, and the elements in group 17 are reactive nonmetals. The periodic table gets its name because these different chemical properties occur regularly, or periodically.

The elements in each group also have the same number of **electrons** in their outer shell. The elements in group 18 all have their outer shells filled with as many electrons as possible. This makes them very stable and unreactive.

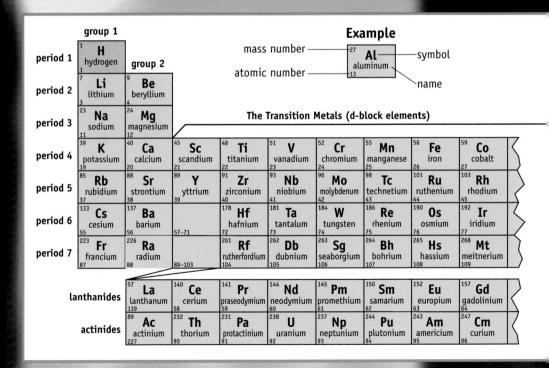

All the elements in group 18 are very unreactive nonmetals. However, the properties of the nonmetals change gradually as you go down the group. They are all gases at room temperature, but their boiling points increase steadily as the elements get larger, and their atoms increase in size as you go down the group.

Group 18 and neon

In this book, you are going to find out all about helium, neon, and the other elements in group 18, as well as their uses and the **compounds** they make.

▼ *This is the periodic table of the elements. All the elements in group 18 are nonmetals. These include helium, neon, argon, krypton, xenon, and radon (the noble gases).*

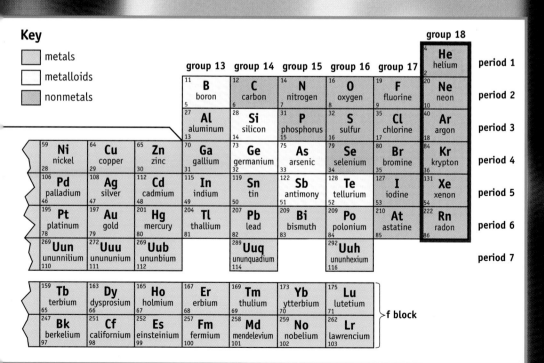

Elements of Group 18

The **elements** in group 18 are all colorless, unreactive gases. They are usually called the noble gases because chemists imagined that they did not **react** with other elements, but stayed alone. However, chemists have now succeeded in making **compounds** with nearly all of them. Most of the elements in the group were discovered or first isolated by a Scottish chemist named Sir William Ramsay.

4 **He** helium 2	**helium** *symbol: He • atomic number: 2 • nonmetal*

Helium is the second most common element in the universe after hydrogen. About 23 percent of the mass of the universe is helium, and about 75 percent is hydrogen. Incredibly, all the other elements together make up just 2 percent of the mass of the universe, so you might imagine that Earth is brimming full of helium. However, most of the helium (and hydrogen) in the universe is found far away in stars like our Sun. Very little is found on the planets. Just 0.00052 percent of Earth's atmosphere is helium, and the proportion in rocks is a thousand times less than that. Also, helium is constantly escaping from the atmosphere into space!

Helium was discovered in 1895. It is less **dense** than air, meaning that balloons filled with helium rise upward. There are no **ores** you can mine to get helium, so most of it is **extracted** from natural gas.

Helium is used in **welding** to keep oxygen away from the metal. It is also used in gas mixtures for divers and hospital patients, and in rockets. People who have breathed in a little helium have a very silly squeaky sound to their voices for a short time!

These spectacular signs are made from neon lights. Different colors are made using other gases, such as argon, or by coatings on the inside of the glass.

20		**neon**
Ne		symbol: Ne • atomic number: 10 • nonmetal
neon		
10		

Neon was discovered in 1898. Like helium, it is very unreactive. About 0.13 percent of the mass of the universe is neon. Although this seems like a small amount, it makes neon the fourth most abundant element in the universe. Neon makes up 0.0018 percent of Earth's atmosphere, but there are no ores you can mine to get it. Neon has to be extracted from air.

Neon is used in **lasers,** and it is the starter gas that warms up orange street lamps when they are first switched on. However, the most familiar use of neon is in brightly colored "neon lights."

40		**argon**
Ar		symbol: Ar • atomic number: 18 • nonmetal
argon		
18		

Argon was discovered in 1894. Only about 0.02 percent of the mass of the universe is argon, but it is the third most abundant gas in Earth's atmosphere (0.934 percent of our air is argon) and the most abundant noble gas in the air. Since argon is extracted from the air, this makes it the cheapest noble gas.

Argon is used whenever a cheap, unreactive atmosphere is needed, such as in electric light bulbs, welding, **refining** titanium, and growing **semiconductor** crystals for use in computer chips.

More Elements of Group 18

84	Kr
	krypton
36	

krypton
symbol: Kr • atomic number: 36 • nonmetal

Krypton (pronounced crip-ton) was discovered in 1898. Just 0.0001 per cent of Earth's atmosphere is krypton, but there are no **ores** you can mine to get krypton, so it is **extracted** from air.

Krypton is an expensive noble gas because it is rare, and this limits its use. Krypton is used in many kinds of bright lights, including fluorescent lights, high-speed photographic lamps, and airport runway lights. Noble gases are usually very unreactive, but scientists have been able to make several krypton compounds. These include a substance called krypton difluoride—but sadly not the glowing green kryptonite of Superman fame!

131	Xe
	xenon
54	

xenon
symbol: Xe • atomic number: 54 • nonmetal

Xenon (pronounced zee-non or zen-non) was discovered in 1898. Barely 0.000001 percent of Earth's atmosphere is xenon. There are no ores of xenon, so it must be extracted from air.

Xenon is used in nuclear physics research, **lasers,** and powerful lights such as lighthouse lamps. Xenon has also been used as an **anesthetic,** but it is too expensive for regular use.

▼ *Krypton and xenon are used in special lamps needed by stroboscopes. Harold Edgerton, an American electrical engineer, developed the high-speed electronic stroboscope in 1931.*

Neil Bartlett, an English-American chemist, made the first noble gas compound in 1962 when he **reacted** xenon, platinum, and fluorine together. Many xenon compounds have been made since then.

| 222 **Rn** radon 86 | **radon** *symbol: Rn • atomic number: 86 • nonmetal* |

Radon (pronounced ray-don) is a very rare **radioactive** gas. It is the **densest** known gas, and it was discovered in 1900 by a German chemist named Friedrich Dorn. He called it radium emanation, but in 1908, William Ramsay called it niton from the Latin word meaning shining. When radon is cooled below −95.8 °F (−71 °C), it turns into a brightly glowing yellow solid, just like you might imagine a radioactive substance should be! At very low temperatures, solid radon becomes orange-red. It has been called radon since 1923.

Radon is extremely rare because it is produced by the radioactive **decay** of other **elements,** such as radium. Some rocks produce radon, and it has been estimated that every square kilometer (0.386 mi^2) of soil to a depth of 6 in. (15 cm) contains around 0.014 oz (0.4 g) of radium, slowly producing the gas. Because radon is radioactive, it can be used to treat cancer. However, high levels of radon can also cause cancer. For instance, people living in houses built over rocks that release radon are at risk of developing cancer.

| 293 **Uuo** ununoctium 118 | **ununoctium** *symbol: Uuo • atomic number: 118 • nonmetal* |

Radon is the last noble gas to occur naturally, and any atoms of the next element in **group** 18 will have to be made artificially. Scientists are very eager to make this element, called ununoctium, to test their theories about **atoms.** Ununoctium (pronounced "yoo-nun-oct-ee-um") is a temporary name that means "one-one-eight," after its **atomic number.** Other artificial elements have been made by bombarding metal targets with high-speed **ions** (atoms missing some **electrons**) in a machine called a particle accelerator. Scientists at the Lawrence Berkeley National Laboratory in California announced that they had made a few atoms of ununoctium in 1999. However, after they did some experiments to check their results, they decided that they had not made the new element after all.

Why Are the Noble Gases So Unreactive?

The noble gases were discovered one after the other very quickly, and it became clear just as quickly that they did not **react** with anything. If a chemical does not react it is **inert,** so the noble gases were also called the inert gases. To understand why the noble gases are so unreactive, it helps to know why other **elements** do react with each other.

It's all about electrons

At the start of the book , you found out that the **electrons** in an **atom** are arranged in shells around the **nucleus.** Some shells can hold more electrons than others, and in general, the farther away the shell is from the nucleus, the more electrons it can hold.

Shell number	Maximum number of electrons allowed in shell	Distance
1	2	close to the nucleus
2	8	
3	18	
4	32	far away from the nucleus

The first shell is closest to the nucleus and can hold only a maximum of two electrons, but the second shell can hold up to eight electrons. The other shells can hold even more electrons, although for argon, potassium, and calcium, the third shell is full when it only contains eight electrons.

In chemistry, we are usually interested in the shell farthest from the nucleus, called the outer shell. If this contains fewer electrons than the maximum number allowed, the atom will react with other atoms so that the outer shell becomes filled. During chemical reactions, atoms fill their outer shells by passing electrons to each other or by sharing them. An atom becomes more stable and less likely to react with other atoms if its outer shell is full.

Passing electrons

Nonmetal atoms are often just one, two, or three electrons short of filling their outer shell. This means that it is best for them to get electrons from another atom to fill their outer shell. Metal atoms are the opposite. They often have just one, two, or three electrons in their outer shell. It is best for them to give these electrons away to another atom to leave the full shell beneath as their new outer shell. When a metal atom gives away electrons, it becomes positively charged. When a nonmetal atom gets extra electrons, it becomes negatively charged. These charged particles are called **ions.** Ions with opposite charges are attracted strongly to each other, and make a chemical **bond** called an ionic bond.

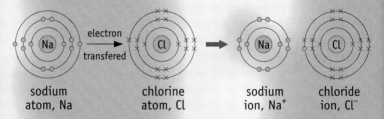

| sodium atom, Na | chlorine atom, Cl | sodium ion, Na⁺ | chloride ion, Cl⁻ |

▲ *Sodium chloride is formed when sodium atoms give away electrons to chlorine atoms. Diagrams like this are called "dot and cross diagrams"—the electrons in each atom are shown differently to make it easier to see how they are given away.*

Sharing electrons

When two nonmetal atoms react with each other, they get so close together that they can share electrons in their outer shells. They usually share just enough electrons to fill their outer shells. When two nonmetal atoms share electrons, they make a chemical bond called a **covalent bond.** Each covalent bond is made from a shared pair of electrons.

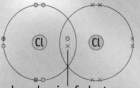

shared pair of electrons

◀ *A chlorine molecule is made from two chlorine atoms joined by a covalent bond. It is usual in these diagrams to show just the outer shells.*

Maximum number of electrons

The outer shells in the noble gases are already full and contain the maximum number of electrons, so the noble gases do not react with other atoms. For most normal purposes, the noble gases are unreactive, or inert.

Trends in Group 18

Most **elements** in the **periodic table** have **atoms** with outer shells that are not completely filled with **electrons.** This means that they will **react** with other elements to form **compounds.** For example, the elements in **group** 17 are very reactive nonmetals such as fluorine and chlorine. They react easily with metals such as sodium and nonmetals such as phosphorus. However, the elements in group 17 become less reactive as you go down their group. A gradual change in a property like chemical reactivity is called a trend.

This is phosphorus burning in chlorine gas to form a compound called phosphorus chloride. Both of these elements are very reactive nonmetals, so the reaction between them is spectacular!

Full electron shells

The noble gases have atoms with outer shells that are already full of electrons. This means that the atoms are stable and do not react with other atoms. Such a lot of energy is needed to add electrons to a full outer shell, or to take them away from it, that the noble gases will react only under very extreme conditions. The noble gases are unreactive, or **inert.** So unlike group 17 and the other groups of elements in the periodic table, it is difficult to see any trend in chemical reactivity going down group 18. However, we can see trends in the physical properties of the elements in group 18, such as their boiling points and the sizes of their atoms.

A lonely existence

Most nonmetal elements are found as **molecules** in which two or more atoms are joined together by **covalent bonds.** All of the elements that are gases at room temperature (except for the noble gases) exist as molecules made from two atoms. These include oxygen, O_2, nitrogen, N_2, fluorine, F_2, and chlorine, Cl_2. The noble gases are very unreactive nonmetals—in fact, they are so unreactive that they do not even react with themselves. This means that they are found as single atoms.

All atoms are tiny, but some are tinier than others

Atoms are so small that scientists usually record their size in a unit called the nanometer. This is given the abbreviation nm, and it is a millionth of a millimeter (0.04 inch). A helium atom is only 0.062 nm in diameter. Sixteen million of them side by side would equal only a millimeter. As you go down the group, the atoms get larger and larger. The biggest atom, radon, is nearly four times bigger than a helium atom. This is because as you go down the group, each atom has more filled electron shells than the last.

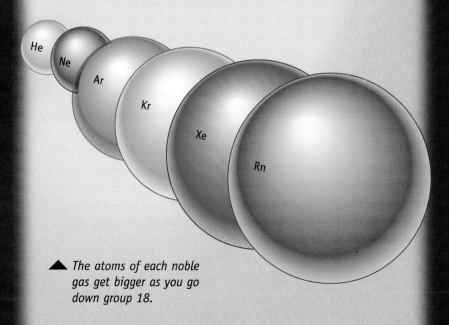

He

Ne

Ar

Kr

Xe

Rn

▲ The atoms of each noble gas get bigger as you go down group 18.

Melting and boiling points

Most nonmetal **elements** exist as simple **molecules.** This means that each molecule is made of only a few **atoms** at most. Simple molecules are attracted to each other by very weak forces between the molecules. The stronger these forces are, the more energy is needed to separate the molecules from each other, and the higher the melting point and boiling point. In general, big molecules have stronger forces between them than small molecules, so they have high melting and boiling points.

The noble gases exist as single atoms. These are small compared to most molecules, so the forces between them are very weak. Their melting and boiling points are so low that they are all gases at room temperature. In **group** 18, helium has the weakest forces between its atoms, so it has the lowest boiling point. Radon has the strongest forces between its atoms, so it has the highest boiling point in group 18.

▼ *This graph shows how the boiling points of the noble gases increase as you go down the group. As you go down the group, the atoms become bigger, and the boiling points of the elements get higher.*

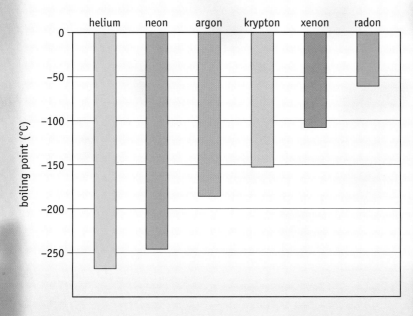

Dense, not thick!

The **density** of a gas at room temperature and pressure depends on the mass of its particles. The heavier the particles are, the denser the gas becomes. The atoms of the elements in group 18 become heavier as you go down the group, and therefore denser, too. Helium has the lightest atoms, so it is the least dense. Radon has the heaviest atoms, so it is more dense—in fact, it is the densest known gas. Helium and neon are less dense than air, so balloons filled with these gases rise. Argon and the remaining noble gases are denser than air, so balloons filled with these gases sink.

◀ *These balloons float upward because they are filled with helium.*

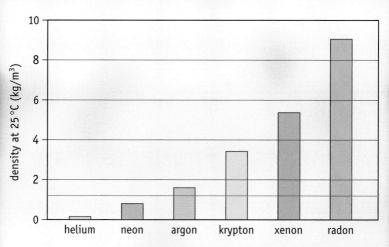

▲ *This graph shows how the densities of the noble gases increase as you go down the group. Helium has the lowest density and radon has the highest density. The red line shows the density of air.*

The Discovery and Isolation of the Noble Gases

Sir William Ramsay, a Scottish chemist, was awarded the Nobel prize for chemistry in 1904 for his work in discovering the noble gases. Despite being rare and unreactive, most of these gases were discovered remarkably quickly, between 1894 and 1900.

Argon

In 1894, the English physicist Lord Rayleigh discovered that nitrogen purified from air was 0.5 percent **denser** than nitrogen made in chemical **reactions.** William Ramsay thought that a dense impurity in air caused the difference, and he set out to find it.

Ramsay removed the oxygen, carbon dioxide, and water vapor from a large sample of air. He then repeatedly passed it over hot magnesium to remove the remaining nitrogen. Eventually, he was left with a small amount of a dense gas, which he quickly realized was a new **element** from a previously unknown **group.** Ramsay called the new element argon, after the Greek word for idle.

▶ *Sir William Ramsay showed that nitrogen and oxygen make up most of the atmosphere. The noble gases make up less than 1 percent of it, with argon being the most abundant of them.*

Helium

In 1868, French astronomer Pierre Janssen discovered helium in the Sun. The way he did this was to study the **spectrum** of the light coming from the Sun during a **solar eclipse.** He found a bright yellow line that everyone thought was caused by sodium, but an English astronomer named Joseph Lockyer realized that it was caused by an unknown element. He called the new element helium, after the Greek word for Sun.

The first sample of helium was isolated by William Ramsay in 1895. He heated a **mineral** called cleveite and **extracted** an unreactive gas that he thought was argon. It took him just two days to show that the gas was not argon, but the same new element that Lockyer had discovered 27 years earlier while investigating the Sun's spectrum.

Neon, krypton, and xenon

Ramsay was left with an interesting problem. He had isolated helium and discovered argon. He knew from their **atomic masses** that these must be the first and third noble gases. In May 1898, Ramsay and his assistant Morris Travers decided to look for the second noble gas in air. They **condensed** argon, using liquid air to cool it down. When they did this, they found that some gas was left above the liquid argon. This was the missing second element. They called it neon, after the Greek word for new.

The race was on to find more noble gases. Ramsay and Travers took some of their sample of neon and cooled it down even more using liquid hydrogen. They managed to isolate another new gas in June 1898, calling it krypton, after the Greek word for hidden. Amazingly, they found yet another gas in July 1898. They called it xenon, after the Greek word for stranger. Within six weeks, they had discovered three new elements!

Radon

In 1900, German chemist Friedrich Dorn discovered a gas coming from a **radioactive** metal called radium. Ramsay and Robert Whytlaw-Gray isolated this extremely rare gas, radon, in 1910.

Light Fantastic

Every **element** produces a different **spectrum** of color when energy is applied to it. For example, when table salt is sprinkled into a Bunsen burner flame, the flame turns orange because of the sodium in the salt. Chemists can figure out what elements there are in many substances by studying the light they produce.

Spectrum of colors

In 1666, Sir Isaac Newton discovered that a **prism** splits white light into a spectrum containing all the colors of the rainbow. The different colors are caused by light waves of different **frequencies.** Red light is caused by waves with low frequencies, and blue light is caused by waves with high frequencies. Green light is in between. Chemicals give off light when energy is applied to them because of the properties of the **electrons** in their **atoms.**

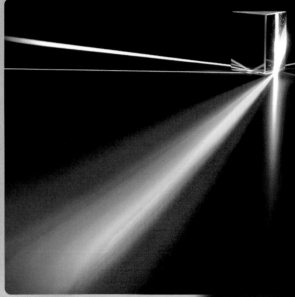

▲ *A prism splits white light up into its spectrum of colors. Red light has the lowest frequency, and blue light has the highest frequency.*

Excited electrons

When energy is applied to an atom, its electrons get excited. They can get so excited that they jump right out of their shell and into a shell farther from the **nucleus.** However, electrons cannot stay excited for long, and they fall back to a shell closer to the nucleus. When they do this, they give off the extra energy as light. The bigger the fall, the higher the frequency of light emitted. Small falls produce light in the red end of the spectrum, but big falls produce light in the blue end of the spectrum. Electrons in different elements can make different jumps and falls, called transitions, so each element produces a different spectrum.

Electric discharge tubes

Electric discharge tubes are clear glass tubes with an electrical contact at each end. If a gas is sealed into the tube at very low pressure, the gas glows when electricity is passed through it. This is because the electricity excites the electrons in the gas so that it emits light. By the end of the 19th century, when the noble gases were being discovered, electric discharge tubes had become extremely useful tools in scientific research, especially for identifying elements. They were the forerunners of the fluorescent light bulb.

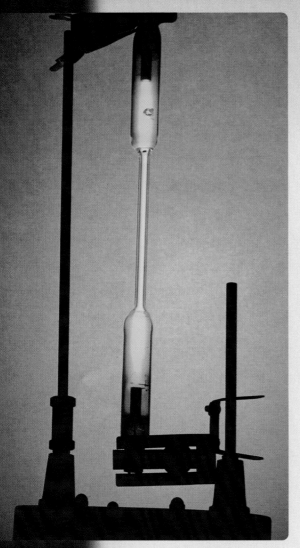

This is an electric discharge tube. It contains mercury vapor at low pressure, which gives off this blue light when electricity is passed through it.

Emission spectra

Chemists use a device called a **spectroscope** to study the light given off by a gas. The spectroscope splits the light into its spectrum, called an emission spectrum. Chemists can study an emission spectrum in detail to see what elements make up the gas. Ramsay and Travers used electric discharge tubes and a spectroscope to help them study the new gases they had discovered. They were able to show very quickly that each of the new gases they had isolated really was a new element, because they all produced different emission spectra. You can see these emission spectra on pages 56 and 57.

Collecting the Noble Gases

The noble gases do not **react** with any other substances under normal conditions, so they form no **compounds** or **ores.** Most are **extracted** from air by cooling it down until it **liquefies** (turns into a liquid), then slowly warming it again. As the liquid warms up, the different gases boil off at different temperatures and are stored in containers ready for use. This is called **fractional distillation** of liquefied air.

Liquefying the air

The air is filtered to remove any dust and smoke. It is also passed through an **alkali** that reacts with any water vapor and carbon dioxide present and removes them. This is because these substances would easily solidify and block the tubes as the air is liquefied.

Air must be cooled to about −200°C (−328 °F) to **condense** most of its gases. You might think that the air is put into a giant refrigerator, but instead it is repeatedly compressed

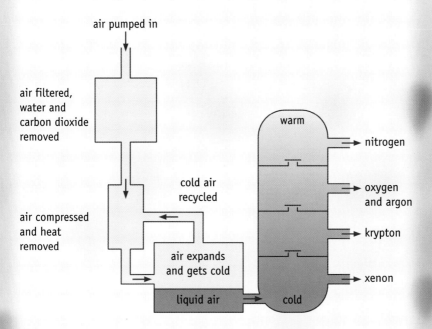

air pumped in

air filtered, water and carbon dioxide removed

air compressed and heat removed

cold air recycled

air expands and gets cold

liquid air

warm

nitrogen

oxygen and argon

krypton

xenon

cold

▲ Fractional distillation of air can extract the noble gases. Neon stays as a gas when the air is liquefied, and is separated from the liquid air. The other gases are piped off at different levels in the fractioning column.

and allowed to expand. Gases heat up when they are compressed or squashed, and cool down when they expand. So the filtered dry air is compressed to about 200 times atmospheric pressure. Heat is produced and escapes through radiators. The air is then allowed to expand, cooling it down. This is done over and over again until most of the air liquefies. The liquid air is then allowed to warm up slowly.

Neon

Neon's boiling point is too low for neon to condense, so it is concentrated in the gas left over when the air turns into a liquid. This gas also contains hydrogen and helium. The hydrogen is removed by burning so that it combines with oxygen to make water. **Activated carbon** is often used in chemistry to remove impurities, and it is used here to remove the helium from the neon gas.

Argon

When the liquefied air warms up, nitrogen boils off first. This is stored because it has a lot of uses. A mixture of oxygen and argon boils off at a slightly higher temperature. The oxygen is removed by passing the mixture over hot copper, and any remaining nitrogen is removed by passing the mixture over hot magnesium. This leaves pure argon.

Krypton and xenon

Krypton and xenon boil off at the highest temperatures. They are passed over hot titanium metal to purify them, and then they are separated from each other by using the distilling process once more.

Helium

Helium can be extracted from natural gas, but many gas fields contain too little helium to make it a worthwhile process. The best gas contains up to 7 percent helium, but gas with over 0.3 percent helium is considered helium-rich. The gas is cooled to liquefy the methane and nitrogen in it, leaving the helium as a gas. The helium is then passed over activated charcoal to remove other gases and impurities, making it up to 99.995 percent pure!

Do Gases Escape into Space?

Earth's atmosphere

Earth's atmosphere is very important to us. Without it, Earth would be as cold and lifeless as the Moon. Two main gases, nitrogen and oxygen, form over 99 percent of Earth's atmosphere. The noble gas argon forms most of the rest, and there are tiny proportions of many other gases as well, including the other **group** 18 **elements.** Why does Earth have an atmosphere and the Moon does not? And why doesn't Earth's atmosphere just escape into space, taking all the noble gases with it? Luckily, we do not need a layer of plastic between Earth and space to stop our atmosphere from leaking away—Earth's gravity stops the speeding gas **molecules** from escaping.

▼ *Nitrogen and oxygen make up most of the atmosphere. The noble gases make up less than 1 percent of it, with argon being the most abundant of them.*

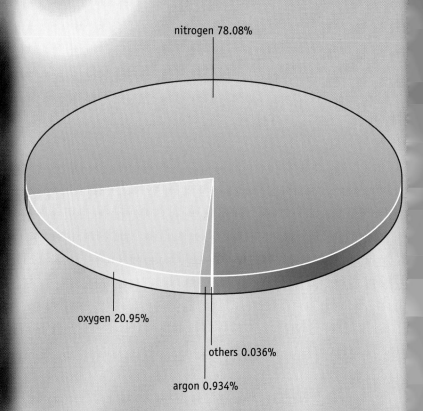

nitrogen 78.08%

oxygen 20.95%

others 0.036%

argon 0.934%

Molecular bumper cars

The molecules in a gas are free to move in all directions, and they can move very quickly. The lightest molecules move the fastest. At room temperature, a radon **atom** would move at 600 ft/sec (183 m/sec), but a helium atom that is 55 times lighter whizzes around at about 4,462 ft/sec (1,360 m/sec). The speed of sound in air is about 1,115 ft/sec (340 m/sec), so a typical helium atom could get from the ground to the International Space Station in less than 5 minutes!

But a particle like an atom or molecule cannot go straight up into space. This is because as it travels, it bumps into other particles. A particle travels less than 0.0000394 inch (0.001 millimeter) before it bumps into another particle, and it has about five billion collisions per second. Earth's gravity also pulls atoms and molecules back toward the ground. The combination of these two effects stops most gases from escaping. The Moon is much smaller than Earth, and its gravity is six times less than Earth's gravity, so if it ever had an atmosphere, that would have escaped long ago.

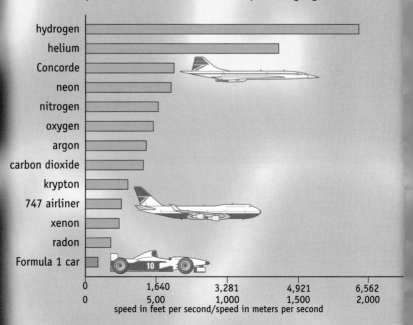

| | 0 | 1,640 | 3,281 | 4,921 | 6,562 |
| | 0 | 5,00 | 1,000 | 1,500 | 2,000 |

speed in feet per second/speed in meters per second

▲ Hydrogen molecules and helium atoms move extremely quickly

A Leaky Atmosphere

To escape Earth's gravity and go into space, an object needs to be traveling at 36,706 ft/sec (11,188 m/sec) or more (about seventeen times faster than Concorde's top speed). A rocket has to accelerate tremendously after take-off so that it goes fast enough to escape Earth's gravity and go into space. When atoms are heated, they gain energy and move more quickly. A helium **atom** in the thermosphere (the upper part of the atmosphere) has a typical speed of 9,842 ft/sec (3,000 m/sec) because it is about 2,192 °F (1,200 °C) there. Other helium atoms are going much faster still. Scientists have learned that if the typical speed of the particles in a gas is a sixth or more of the speed needed to escape, all the gas will escape into space in a billion years. Hydrogen and helium have the smallest particles, so they slowly escape Earth's atmosphere, while all the other gases do not.

▼ This graph shows the different speeds of the **molecules** in a gas. The most probable speed is the typical speed of a molecule in the gas. However, some are going more slowly and some are going more quickly. A tiny number are going faster than the escape velocity and will escape into space.

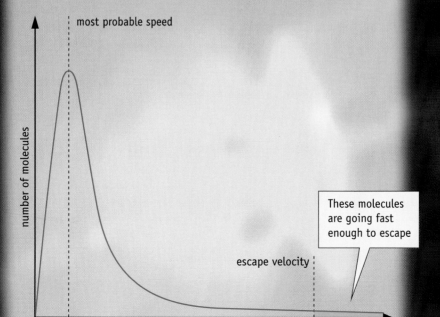

most probable speed

number of molecules

escape velocity

These molecules are going fast enough to escape

A recycler's dream

Neon, argon, krypton, and xenon are the ultimate in recyclable substances. We **extract** them from the air, use them for many things, and then release them unchanged back into the air. They do not escape from the atmosphere into space, so they will always be there for us.

Radon is being produced continually from **radioactive** rocks and is not likely to run out. The area around Amarillo, Texas, has helium-rich gas fields that produce more helium than anywhere else in the world.

Although helium escapes from the atmosphere, this happens only very slowly, so we should be able to recycle it from the air in the same way as the other noble gases. However, this would be much more expensive than extracting it from natural gas because there is so little of it in the air. To avoid running out of relatively cheap helium, the United States government keeps a stockpile of nearly a 1.31 billion cubic yards (1 billion cubic meters) of helium!

◄ *The atmosphere of the planet Neptune is 83 percent hydrogen, 15 percent helium, and 2 percent methane.*

Radioactivity and the Noble Gases

Atoms of an **element** always have the same number of **protons** in their **nucleus.** For example, helium atoms always have two protons, and krypton atoms always have 36 protons. However, they do not always have the same number of **neutrons** in their nucleus.

Isotopes

Isotopes are atoms of an element that have the same number of protons and **electrons,** but different numbers of **neutrons.** The most abundant or common isotope of helium is helium-4. This has two protons and two neutrons in its nucleus, and it is given the chemical symbol $^4_2$He. About 0.000137 percent of helium atoms are another isotope, helium-3, or $^3_2$He. This has two protons but only one neutron in its nucleus. Some elements have lots of different isotopes. Xenon has nearly 30!

> ## Chemical symbols
> *In a chemical symbol like $^4_2$He or $^3_2$He, the bottom number is the **atomic number.** It shows how many protons there are in the nucleus. The top number is the **mass number,** and it shows the number of protons and the number of neutrons. If you want to find out how many neutrons there are in the nucleus, just subtract the bottom number from the top number!*

Half-life

The nucleus of an atom can break up or **decay** into smaller pieces. It is not possible to predict when an individual atom will decay, but by studying huge numbers of atoms, it is possible to say how long it takes for half of them to decay. This time is called the **half-life** of the atom, and it never changes. It remains unaffected by heating, cooling, or **reacting** atoms with other elements. Some isotopes have a very unstable nucleus, and their half-lives are only a fraction of a second. Other isotopes have a more stable nucleus. Their half-lives may be thousands or millions of years.

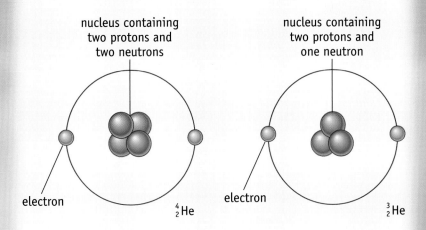

nucleus containing
two protons and
two neutrons

nucleus containing
two protons and
one neutron

electron

electron

$^{4}_{2}\text{He}$

$^{3}_{2}\text{He}$

▲ These diagrams show the atoms of two helium
isotopes. Both atoms contain two protons in the
nucleus and two electrons in the shell around it.
However, helium-4 atoms ($^{4}_{2}\text{He}$) have two neutrons in
the nucleus and helium-3 atoms ($^{3}_{2}\text{He}$) have only one
neutron in the nucleus.

The dangers of an unstable nucleus

When an unstable nucleus breaks up, it decays to become
another isotope of the same element or an isotope of
another element. **Radiation** is given out in this process.
There are different types of radiation, each with a different
penetrating power. **Alpha (a) radiation** consists of helium
nuclei moving at about a tenth the speed of light, and it is
stopped by paper. **Beta (b) radiation** consists of electrons
produced by a nucleus when it breaks up; it travels through
paper and thin sheets of aluminum (less than 0.12 in., or
0.3 cm, thick). **Gamma (g) radiation** is a type of high-
energy light, like X-rays but more powerful, that can travel
through paper, aluminum, and thin sheets of lead. It may
need several meters of concrete or very thick lead to stop it.

If radiation damages the DNA in our cells, it can lead to
cancer. There are strict laws to protect us from overexposure
to **radioactive** chemicals. Of the noble gases, helium, radon,
and argon have some particularly interesting links with
radioactivity. These are explored on the next pages.

Alpha Particles, Emanations, and Old Dates

Helium and alpha particles

Ernest Rutherford, a British physicist born in New Zealand, investigated the **radiation** produced by radium and uranium. He won the 1908 Nobel prize for chemistry for his work on **radioactivity.**

Rutherford found that there were three types of radiation. He called these **alpha, beta,** and **gamma radiation.** He discovered that radioactive substances produced gases, called "emanations." These emanations were chemically unreactive, and Rutherford believed that they contained noble gases. In 1903, working with an English chemist named Frederick Soddy, Rutherford collected some emanation from radium bromide. When they studied the emission **spectrum** of the emanation, they found that the gas was indeed helium.

In another experiment in 1908, Rutherford found that alpha radiation fired into an empty glass container turned into helium gas. By making careful measurements, he discovered that alpha radiation is a stream of fast-moving helium **atoms** stripped of their **electrons.** These particles come from the **nuclei** of unstable **isotopes** when they break apart during radioactive **decay.** It turns out that helium is being made constantly by the radioactive decay of unstable isotopes in rocks such as granite. Just enough helium seems to be made to balance the losses from the atmosphere.

New Zealand-born ▶
physicist Lord Rutherford
(1871–1937) is considered
to be the father of
nuclear physics.

Thorium emanation and radon

Rutherford and Soddy also studied the radiation coming off a metal called thorium. They found that it produced a gas that they called thorium emanation, or thoron. It was an intensely radioactive gas, and they were able to show in 1902 that it was radon, the noble gas discovered just two years before. At one time, radon had several names because it had been discovered in different ways at about the same time! Radon is very rare because it is formed when **elements** with very large nuclei decay in nuclear **reactions,** and these elements themselves are rare.

*Nuclear reactions are not like chemical reactions. In chemical reactions the elements join to each other, or **bond,** in different ways using their electrons. However, in nuclear reactions, the nucleus splits to make new elements. The word equation below shows a nuclear reaction to produce radon and alpha particles (helium nuclei) from radium.*

radium-226 $\rightarrow$ radon-222 + alpha particle

Potassium-argon dating

Potassium is a very common metal found in many **compounds** in rocks. Potassium-40, $^{40}_{19}K$, is a radioactive isotope that decays slowly to argon-40, $^{40}_{18}Ar$. If a rock contains potassium, scientists can figure out its age by using the **half-life** of potassium-40 and comparing the amount of the two isotopes in it. Young rocks have more potassium-40 than argon-40, and older rocks have more argon-40 than potassium-40. The method allows rocks that are between a hundred thousand years and four billion years old to be dated accurately. However, if the rocks melt at all, the argon in them escapes and resets the clock!

CHAPTER 3

Helium

Party balloons and airships are filled with helium, but the gas has many other uses. It is used in medicine, by divers, in **lasers,** and for many complex tasks.

Mixtures for breathing

If you have ever been swimming in the sea, you might have used a mask and a short breathing tube called a snorkel to look at all the interesting things below the surface. You cannot go very deep with a snorkel because the pressure on your chest becomes too great for you to breathe. If you want to dive deeper, you need to use compressed air. This air, stored under pressure in tanks, is pushed into the diver's lungs through a mouthpiece. Unfortunately, compressed air causes problems in very deep dives.

▼ *These divers can breathe underwater because they have taken a supply of air with them. It is compressed into metal tanks carried on their backs.*

If oxygen and nitrogen are breathed in under pressure while underwater, they can lead to dangerous symptoms. Oxygen can cause "oxygen poisoning," producing twitches and fits. Nitrogen can cause "nitrogen sickness, producing symptoms similar to drinking too much alcohol. Divers can also have problems when they return to the surface. The pressure underwater causes nitrogen to dissolve in the diver's blood. If the diver returns to the surface too quickly, the decrease in pressure releases the nitrogen, forming bubbles—a bit like taking the top off a bottle of soda after shaking it. Small blood vessels become blocked by these bubbles, causing terrible pain called the "bends." Diluting the breathing gas with helium helps to avoid these problems.

Heliox is a mixture of 80 percent helium and 20 percent oxygen, and it is used for deep dives. Divers also use a mixture of helium, oxygen, and nitrogen called trimix. Helium does not have the same effect as oxygen and nitrogen under pressure, and it does not dissolve easily in the blood. As the amount of oxygen and nitrogen in the breathing mixture is reduced, divers are less likely to suffer oxygen poisoning or nitrogen sickness. They can also return to the surface more quickly after a long dive. But there is one strange side effect—a squeaky voice!

Squeaky sounds!

People who take a breath of helium quickly discover that they sound like Donald Duck for a short time. When we speak, air is pushed over our vocal cords. This causes them to vibrate, and the faster they vibrate, the higher the **pitch** they make. We can change the pitch of our voice by using muscles to tighten our vocal cords, but the pitch is also modified by the size and shape of our throat and mouth. Children have short throats that select sound waves with high **frequencies,** so they have high-pitched voices. Adults have longer throats, so they have deeper voices. Helium is less **dense** than air, so the speed of sound is two and a half times higher in helium than it is in air. This means that the loudest vibrations in our throat and mouth are about two and a half octaves higher in pure helium than they are in air.

Helium, Hydrogen, and the *Hindenburg*

A quart (0.95 liter) of air at room temperature and pressure has a mass of 0.04 oz (1.2 g), but that much helium has a mass of just 0.0059 oz (0.166 g). This means that a liter plastic bottle filled with helium will be about 0.035 oz (1 g) less than one filled with air. If the mass of the plastic itself were less than 0.035 oz (1 g), the bottle would float upward! Usually the plastic will have a greater mass than this, but balloons are made from much thinner material and may easily have a low enough mass to float when filled with helium. A helium balloon 3.3 feet (1 meter) in diameter could lift over 1.1 lb (0.5kg), including the mass of the balloon.

Weather balloons

Meteorologists use weather balloons filled with helium to collect information about the atmosphere to help them with their weather forecasts. Large balloons about 10 feet (3 meters) in diameter can carry an instrument called a **radiosonde** high into the air. Radiosondes measure pressure, temperature, humidity, and more, transmitting the data to ground stations. The balloons are not completely filled on take-off, so they have a teardrop shape. As they rise into the sky, the air pressure goes down and the helium inside them expands. They eventually burst, and the instruments fall back to the ground using a parachute. Helium **molecules** are so small that special materials have to be used for the balloons. If ordinary rubber is used, the helium can quickly escape through tiny holes (called pores) in the rubber.

A scientist releases a weather balloon in Antarctica.

In World War II, tethered balloons like this were used to protect industrial centers from hostile aircraft. In bad weather, kites were sent up instead.

Airships

It is possible to carry very large masses into the sky if huge balloons are used. Before helium was readily available, hydrogen was used. Hydrogen is actually slightly better than helium at lifting balloons, but it is extremely **flammable** and can cause explosions. In World War II, barrage balloons filled with over 654 yd^3 (500 m^3) of hydrogen made it more difficult for enemy aircraft to fly over towns and cities. However, these balloons were tiny compared to the giant airships.

The most famous airship was the *Hindenburg*, built with an aluminum frame to keep its shape and completed in Germany in 1936. The *Hindenburg* was 804 ft (245 m) long (over three times longer than a Boeing 747), 134.5 ft (41 m) in diameter, and was filled with 248,511 yd^3 (190,000 m^3) of hydrogen. It could carry 50 crew, 72 passengers, and 11 tons of cargo at speeds of up to 75 mph (120 kph).

While trying to land in 1937, the *Hindenburg* burst into flames and was completely destroyed, killing many of the people on board. The hydrogen gas that filled the balloon was blamed for the accident, and airships went out of style for a long time. It now seems that it was the coating painted on the fabric that caused the fire. However, modern airships are much smaller and use nonflammable helium to lift them.

Helium the Super Gas

It is important to keep reactive gases such as oxygen away when growing **semiconductor** crystals for computer chips, or when **welding** metals such as steel. Helium is often used to provide an unreactive atmosphere in these processes, avoiding **reactions** that could damage the semiconductor crystals or welded metal. Helium also conducts heat extremely well, and its low **density** and unreactivity make it ideal for some very complex applications.

Rocket science

Rocket motors often use liquid hydrogen for fuel, and liquid oxygen to make the fuel burn in space. Once the motor starts, the high-pressure exhaust gas thrusts the rocket forward, but it also tries to push the liquid hydrogen and oxygen back up the pipes and into their storage tanks. The simplest way to avoid this is to use helium under high pressure. Helium is chosen for several reasons. It stays as a gas at very low temperatures, and it forces the liquids into the motor without dissolving in them or reacting with them.

Leak testing

If you have tried to mend a flat bicycle tire, you will probably have held the inner tube under water to watch for bubbles and find where the air is leaking out.

Testing for leaks is very important in industry, especially testing containers that might hold dangerous sul Helium is ideal for leak-testing because it does not react with materials, and its **atoms** are very small compared to the **molecules** of every other gas. This means it can pass through even the tiniest gaps. A device called a **mass spectrometer** is used to analyze the air around the object being tested to see if any helium has escaped. Helium leak-testing is ten thousand times more sensitive than other methods, such as ultrasonic testing. It can detect leaks of just one drop of water per year!

A pressurized container of liquid helium. ▶

This liquid-fuel engine for the Ariane-5 spacecraft uses liquid hydrogen and liquid oxygen. Liquid helium keeps the liquid oxygen under pressure, while pressurized helium gas is used to work valves and adjust the direction of the engine during the rocket's flight.

Wind tunnels

Wind tunnels are used to simulate the flow of air over bridges, buildings, cars, and aircraft to check their design. High-speed air is forced over the object if it is small, or over an accurate model if the real object is large. Streams of smoke are often used to show the airflow over the object, but soap bubbles filled with helium are often used instead. These do not sink to the ground like ordinary bubbles, so they flow over the model in the currents of air. Pulses of **laser** light are shone into the stream of bubbles to make them show up, and to let the engineers check the speed of the air.

If very high-speed supersonic tests on models are needed, it becomes very difficult to use air. Water droplets may form in the airflow, ruining the experiment, and the air rushing over the model can produce enough heat to damage it. Using helium instead of air reduces these problems and allows speeds of up to 20 times the speed of sound to be tested.

Helium the Super Fluid

Helium must be cooled to a very low temperature before it will **liquefy.** It has the lowest melting point of any **element,** and will turn into a liquid only below −452.02 °F (−268.9 °C). Liquid helium cannot be solidified at normal atmospheric pressure, and it has some other very strange properties apart from being very cold.

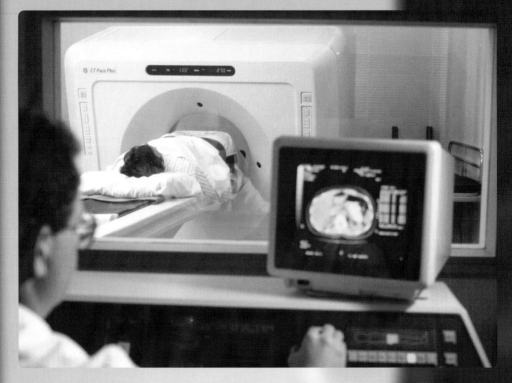

▲ An MRI scanner uses superconducting magnets cooled by liquid helium to produce very detailed images of the inside of the body.

Liquid helium the refrigerant

Liquid helium is extremely cold and unreactive, so it is very useful as a refrigerant to produce very low temperatures. Equipment can be cooled to −320.8 °F (−196 °C) using liquid nitrogen as the refrigerant, but liquid helium can cool down equipment much further. At temperatures this low—close to the lowest possible temperature, known as **absolute zero** (−459.67 °F/−273.15 °C)—strange things start to happen.

Metals are good conductors of electricity, but they all resist the flow of electricity to some extent. Some energy is usually lost as heat, but at very low temperatures metals become **superconductors.** This means that they no longer resist the flow of electricity. Superconductors are used in sophisticated electronic devices such as sensitive microwave detectors, and electricity cables. Cables made from superconductors carry electricity without losing any energy as heat.

Superfluid helium

Ordinary liquid helium is called helium I (helium one). If this is cooled below −455.8 °F (−271 °C), it turns into a weird liquid called helium II (helium two). This liquid is **superfluid** helium, first discovered in 1934 by Russian physicist Peter Kapitza. Helium II has no **viscosity** at all, so it is extremely runny. It flows easily through tiny holes that helium I would not be able to get through, and it forms a thin film of helium that crawls over surfaces and out of containers.

Most substances contract when they get colder, but helium II expands when it is cooled. It conducts heat three million times better than helium I, and instead of flowing from warm areas to cold areas, helium II flows the opposite way. Liquid helium is the only liquid than cannot be solidified just by cooling. Solid helium is made from the liquid by cooling it to within 1.8 °F (1 °C) of absolute zero under at least 25 times atmospheric pressure. Liquid helium is used in low-temperature physics research.

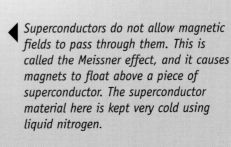

Superconductors do not allow magnetic fields to pass through them. This is called the Meissner effect, and it causes magnets to float above a piece of superconductor. The superconductor material here is kept very cold using liquid nitrogen.

Neon

Liquid neon may be used instead of liquid helium in some low-temperature devices. It is cheaper than helium and it has more refrigerating capacity. Neon is a colorless gas, but it glows bright red when electricity is passed through it, so it is used in **lasers** and the brightly colored neon lights used for advertising signs.

From barometers to electric discharge tubes

Barometers are devices that measure atmospheric pressure. Mercury barometers are made from a tube, closed at the top, that contains mercury and is held over a dish of mercury. The higher the air pressure, the farther up the tube the mercury is pushed. French astronomer Jean Picard discovered in 1675 that an empty mercury barometer tube glowed faintly when it was shaken. Static electricity caused by the shaking made the mercury vapor produce light. By accident, Picard had discovered a primitive electric discharge tube. This is a device that contains a gas at low pressure and glows when high voltage electricity is passed through it. The gas glows because the electricity excites the **electrons** in it so that they emit light.

Several thousand volts—and a pressure of about a thousandth of an atmosphere—are needed to get a really bright glow. This meant that the development of practical electric discharge tubes had to wait until the late 19th century, when efficient electricity generators and vacuum pumps became widely available. There were many designs of lamps based on the electric discharge tube, and the neon light was invented in 1902 by Georges Claude, a French chemist and engineer. The public first saw Claude's neon lights in 1910 when he displayed one in Paris.

Neon lights

Neon lights are so bright that they can be seen in daylight, and at night they are spectacular. The basic color of a neon light in a clear glass tube is red, but you will see lots of other colors as well. Over a hundred different colors can be produced by using colored glass, or by coating the inside of

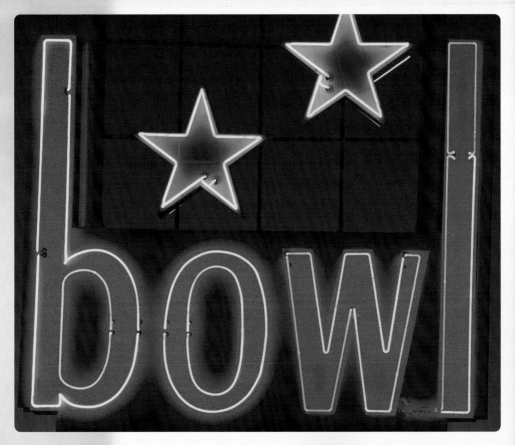

▲ *Neon lights are used to make bright advertising signs like this. Glass tubes are bent into the desired shape before the gas is added to complete the neon lights.*

the glass tube with chemicals called **phosphors.** Sometimes the "neon" light does not contain neon at all. The brilliant blue "neon" lights actually contain a mixture of argon and mercury instead of neon.

Different shapes are made by heating the glass tube in a flame and bending it before the gas is added. Animated signs are made by using several neon lights, and arranging each one to flash on and off in sequence. A typical neon light needs between 2000 V and 15,000 V to light it, so a **transformer** is used to increase the normal voltage supplied to these levels. Narrow glass tubes can be used to get a really intense light, but these need a higher voltage than wider tubes. Very small neon lights are often used in electronic equipment to show whether a device is on or off.

Helium-neon Lasers

"**Laser**" stands for Light Amplification by Stimulated Emission of **Radiation.** Lasers produce very intense beams of light that do not spread out very much. Although it would be too faint for you to see, a laser beam shining onto the Moon (238,855 mi/384,400 km) away) would spread by only 3.7 mi (6 km). This is like shining a flashlight on a wall 32.8 ft (10 m) away, with its beam spreading by just 0.0059 in. (0.15 mm)! Ali Javan, an Irani-born American physicist, built the first helium-neon laser in 1961. This laser was the first to produce a continuous beam of light, rather than short flashes.

A little laser lesson

A gas laser is made from a tube with mirrors at each end facing each other. The mixture of gases inside is at low pressure, and often contains up to twelve times more helium than neon. Electrodes inside the tube power the laser light. About 10,000 V may be needed to start the laser, but only about 2,000 V are needed to keep it going.

When the electricity passes through the gas mixture in the laser, it excites the **electrons** in the **atoms** and makes them jump into shells farther from the **nucleus.** The helium atoms get most of the energy because there are more of them, but they pass some of the energy on to the neon atoms. When the excited electrons in the neon atoms drop down to shells closer to the nucleus, they lose their extra energy and give off light. The light is reflected over and over again between the two mirrors, quickly increasing its intensity and producing a strong beam of light from one end of the laser. The laser light usually has a wavelength of 632.8 nanometers, which we see as bright red light. This red laser light has many familiar uses.

Barcodes and doctors

Most items bought from stores have barcodes on the packaging. Each unique barcode is a pattern of black and white stripes of different widths. The barcode is scanned using a beam of light, usually from a helium-neon laser. The black bars absorb a lot of the light, while the white bars reflect most of it. This means that the sensor in the barcode reader

This helium-neon laser produces its characteristic red light, although other colors are also available from modern lasers.

gets a varying pattern of light intensity passed back to it, from which a computer can figure out the barcode. The clerk may have problems scanning barcodes printed on transparent plastic because the laser light goes through the plastic instead of being reflected back to the sensor.

Surgeons may use a laser that produces **infrared** light to remove moles and warts, and as a laser scalpel. We cannot see infrared light, so help is needed to aim the laser in the right direction! Helium-neon lasers can provide a red dot that can be used to aim the infrared laser. Helium-neon lasers are also used by lecturers to point at their slides and computer presentations in lecture halls, as well as by surveyors, construction workers, and scientists doing research.

CHAPTER 5

Argon

Argon is colorless, but it glows bright blue when electricity is passed through it, so it is used in "neon" lights used for advertising signs. Like the other noble gases, argon is an unreactive gas. However, scientists from the University of Helsinki in Finland created an argon **compound** called argon fluorohydride, HArF, at the beginning of this century. They did this by freezing a mixture of hydrogen fluoride and argon, then shining **ultraviolet** light on it. Unfortunately, the **molecules** of HArF broke apart as they warmed up from −446.08 °F (−265.6 °C) and bumped into each other!

Lightbulbs

Ordinary incandescent lightbulbs contain a filament made from very fine tungsten wire. The wire heats up when electricity is passed through it. It gets so hot—about 5,432 °F (3,000 °C)—that it glows brightly. The filament is made from tungsten because this has a very high melting point and will not melt with the heat. However, it will **react** with oxygen in the air, so it has to be surrounded by a glass bulb with the air removed. If the filament is in a vacuum, the metal slowly evaporates while the bulb is in use, turning the glass black. A small amount of argon, or argon mixed with nitrogen, is added to the vacuum in the bulb. The gas mixture stops the tungsten from evaporating so quickly, and of course does not react with it.

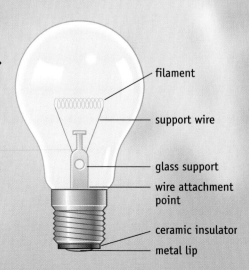

In a typical incandescent lightbulb, the glass envelope contains argon, or a mixture of argon and nitrogen, to slow down the evaporation of the tungsten filament.

filament

support wire

glass support

wire attachment point

ceramic insulator

metal lip

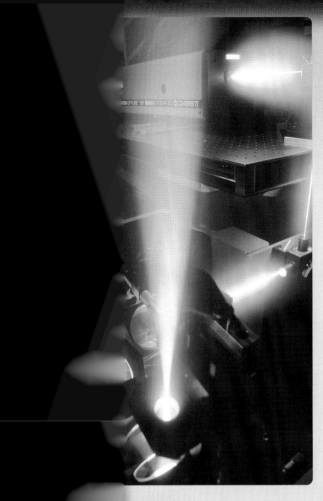

◀ *This argon laser produces a blue green laser light. It is being used here to make fine adjustments to some scientific equipment.*

Argon lasers

Neon **lasers** produce red light, but argon lasers produce blue green light. The intensity of the light beam determines the power of the laser. Among their many uses in science and medicine, argon laser beams can be used to remove stains from teeth, producing startlingly white teeth. Cosmetic surgeons use argon lasers to reduce or remove birthmarks without damaging the normal skin around them. Ophthalmic surgeons use argon lasers to treat eye problems. High-power beams are used to treat growths in the retina, and low-power beams are used to repair torn or damaged retinas. A range of lasers called excimer lasers use fluorine gas mixed with argon to produce beams of ultraviolet light. These can be used to correct the vision of nearsighted patients by removing tiny, carefully calculated amounts of the cornea from the eye.

Inert atmospheres

Argon is the most abundant noble gas in the air, so it is the cheapest noble gas. Despite the success of scientists in creating HArF, argon is very useful for providing a relatively cheap unreactive, or **inert,** atmosphere. Argon atmospheres keep oxygen away from metals while they are being **welded** or cut with a cutting torch, and they protect **semiconductor** crystals while they are being grown. An argon atmosphere can also help produce some metals from their **ores,** such as titanium, a strong, low-**density** metal used in aircraft and artificial hip joints.

Krypton

Krypton is an unreactive gas, but chemists have managed to make several **compounds** of krypton, including krypton difluoride, KrF_2. This is a solid made by cooling a mixture of krypton and fluorine to -320.8 °F (-196 °C) using liquid nitrogen, then bombarding it with X-rays. The **bonds** between the **atoms** break at room temperature, so krypton difluoride is very unlikely to live up to the reputation of "kryptonite" established in the *Superman* comic books!

Lightbulbs

The tungsten filament in an ordinary lightbulb gradually evaporates in use, blackening the glass bulb and eventually becoming so thin that it breaks. Argon is often used to reduce the rate of evaporation. However, Hungarian scientist Imre Bródy discovered in 1930 that krypton works better. For a given light output, a lightbulb filled with krypton can be made smaller than one filled with argon, so flashlights often use krypton bulbs. Lightbulbs filled with krypton are more efficient, since they convert more electricity into light rather than heat. The filament inside can be allowed to get hotter without reducing its life too much, and this produces a very white light. Krypton bulbs are much more expensive than ordinary bulbs because krypton itself is very expensive.

A flash in the dark

Krypton is used in specialized devices called stroboscopes. These produce a bright light that can be made to flash on and off very quickly. The bulbs in a stroboscope work in a similar way to neon lights. However, a very large current of electricity is passed through the krypton in a very short burst that lasts only a fraction of a second, producing a flash of white light. Engineers use stroboscopes to measure the speed of spinning machinery. When the speed of the flashes matches the speed of the machine, the machine looks like it has stopped. This also allows the engineers to see if any moving parts look damaged, without needing to turn the machine off.

Double glazing

Considerable amounts of heat can be lost from buildings through glass windows. For example, if a building is kept at 68 °F (20 °C) above the outside temperature, as in winter, a pane of glass 1.2 yards square (1 meter square) lets about 120 W of heat energy through it, increasing the heating bill. Double glazing the windows can often help—and in very cold climates, even triple glazing is used. Typical double glazing (with air in the gap between the two panes of glass) reduces heat loss by about 53 percent compared to a single pane of glass. If the gap is filled with krypton, the heat loss is reduced by 64 percent. The lower heat loss means that less **fossil fuel** is needed to heat the building. This reduces the fuel bill and saves on a **nonrenewable** resource, but the krypton makes the windows more expensive than usual.

▼ Stroboscope lamps contain krypton. They can be flashed on and off very quickly, "freezing" the action like this.

CHAPTER 7

Xenon

Like the other noble gases, xenon is colorless, tasteless, and unreactive. However, the first noble gas **compound** was a xenon compound called xenon hexafluoroplaninate, $XePtF_6$, made by British chemist Neil Bartlett in 1962. Chemists have been able to make many other xenon compounds since then. Many of them are powerful **oxidizing agents.** This means that they can remove **electrons** from other substances, so scientists use them in their research.

Bubble chambers

Liquid xenon can be used in a bubble chamber, a device physicists use to detect high-energy **subatomic particles.** The pressure in the bubble chamber is adjusted so that the liquid xenon is just about ready to boil. Wherever the particles pass though the liquid xenon, they give it just enough energy to boil. Trails of tiny bubbles of xenon gas form as the particles pass through. The physicists can photograph these and use the images in their research.

Xenon compounds

Xenon fluorides are all white solids at room temperature. Xenon difluoride, XeF_2, is made when equal volumes of xenon and fluorine are heated together to about 572 °F (300 °C). Xenon tetrafluoride, XeF_4, and xenon hexafluoride, XeF_6, are made if there is more fluorine than xenon, and the mixture is heated under pressure. These compounds react with water to make xenon trioxide, XeO_3, an explosive white solid! Xenon tetraoxide, XeO_4, is also explosive, but $XeOF_4$ is a stable, colorless liquid.

Fluorine is a very reactive gas that is difficult to store and handle, and xenon difluoride can be used as a safer source of fluorine for chemical reactions. When they are heated, crystals of xenon difluoride break down again to form xenon and fluorine. The fluorine formed by heating xenon difluoride can be used during the manufacture of computer chips to remove tiny amounts of silicon from the chips. It will also convert a chemical called uracil into fluoro-uracil, a kind of anticancer chemical.

Lasers and lighthouses

High-pressure xenon arc lamps produce **ultraviolet** light that can kill bacteria. Xenon excimer **lasers** are used in medicine and, just like krypton, xenon is used in stroboscopes and flash bulbs. Xenon lamps can produce brilliant flashes of light just a few millionths of a second long, and are used in lighthouses. Smeaton Eddystone, the world's first modern stone lighthouse, was built in 1756 near Plymouth, England. It took just 24 candles to power it, but modern xenon lamps shine with the power of 20 million candles and can be seen over 62 mi (100 km) away!

Into space with a blue glow

Xenon is the fuel used in an advanced engine system for space probes, called the xenon-ion propulsion system. Electrons are removed from the xenon **atoms** to make positively charged xenon **ions** (just as in the electric discharge tubes). These ions stream out of the engine at 18.6 mi/sec (30 km/sec), accelerating the probe while using only 4.59 oz (130 g) of fuel a day.

▼ *A xenon-ion propulsion system emits a blue glow.*

CHAPTER 8

Radon

Radon is intensely **radioactive.** It is a colorless gas at room temperature. When it is cooled to –95.8 °F (–71 °C), it becomes a solid with a soft yellow glow. As the solid radon is cooled down even more, it becomes an orange-red color. Like the other noble gases, radon is unreactive, but chemists have been able to make radon difluoride, RnF_2.

▼ *Volcanologists collect gas samples from the rim of the Colima Volcano's crater in Colombia. It is an active volcano—when it erupted in 1993, six scientists and three local people were killed.*

What's in a name?

Radon is formed when radioactive **elements decay.** Even though it is the rarest noble gas, it was discovered more than once. This meant that, for a while, radon had several names.

Friedrich Dorn found radon first in 1900 by studying a radioactive metal called radium. He called the gas "radium emanation" because it came from, or emanated from, radium. Two years later, Ernest Rutherford and Frederick Soddy discovered it coming from another radioactive metal called thorium, so they called it "thorium emanation" or "thoron." In 1904, Friedrich Giesel and André Debierne discovered the gas coming from yet another radioactive metal called actinium. This gas was called "actinium emanation" or "actinon." When William Ramsay and Robert Whytlaw-Gray finally isolated the element and measured its **density** in 1908, they called it "niton"—yet another name!

Eventually it became clear that the different emanations were the three natural **isotopes** of the same element. Radium emanation is radon-222, thoron is radon-220, and actinon is radon-219. The name niton never really caught on, and the element has been called radon since 1923. The names thoron and actinon are still sometimes used as common names for radon-220 and radon-219. When they are used in this way, the name radon means radon-222.

*This table shows the **half-lives** of the three natural isotopes of radon. When these isotopes decay, they give off **alpha radiation** and produce a radioactive metal called polonium. $^{219}_{86}Rn$ decays so quickly that barely 0.1 percent of it is left after 40 seconds!*

isotope	half-life
$^{222}_{86}$ Rn	3.82 days
$^{220}_{86}$ Rn	55.6 seconds
$^{219}_{86}$ Rn	3.96 seconds

Radon and Radiation

Radon seeds

Like radon itself, the **elements** made when it **decays** are also very **radioactive.** This means that radon gas can kill cancer cells if used correctly. It would be very dangerous just to let a patient breathe in radon and hope for the best. Instead, the radon gas is sealed into tiny gold or glass tubes called seeds. These are then put into the cancerous growth by a doctor. If the seed is placed correctly, the **radiation** from it kills only the nearby cancer cells in the growth and not the healthy cells in the rest of the body.

The radon comes from radium, or a radium **compound** dissolved in water. It is collected every few days by pumping the gas off and sealing it into a seed. Very little radon is collected from the radium, but only a little is needed. Today, there are other ways to use radiation to treat cancer, so radon seeds are very unlikely to be used now.

▼ *Modern radiotherapy uses machines called linear accelerators, rather than radon seeds. The machine is lined up using a harmless **laser** beam as a guide. Then radiation, such as X-rays, is aimed at the cancer.*

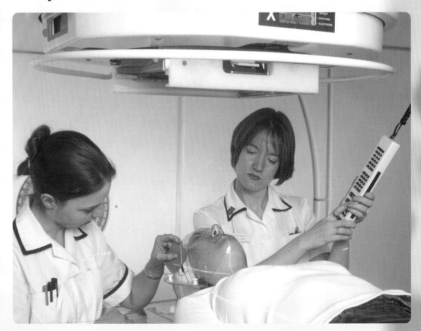

Background radiation

We are all exposed to a small amount of natural **background radiation.** This is caused by cosmic rays from space, our food and drink, and radioactive substances found in the air, rocks and soil. You cannot avoid this dose of radioactivity, but the typical yearly dose from it is only about 4 mSv (four millisievert, pronounced "milli-see-vert"). Uranium is a radioactive metal found in rocks and soil. It produces radium when it decays, and when the radium decays, it produces radon. The radioactivity from radon causes about half our dose of background radiation, but if a lot of radon gets into our homes, it can add much more.

When the Egyptian Atomic Energy Authority measured the radioactivity caused by radon gas in some ancient monuments, they made a surprise discovery. The air in the pyramids, tombs, and tunnels contained levels of radioactivity up to 25 times higher than the recommended maximum levels! Luckily, the highest radon levels were found in a pyramid that is not open to the public, and of course nobody lives in the pyramids. However, radon can be a big problem if it gets into our homes.

▼ This pie chart shows the typical proportions of the different sources of background radiation.

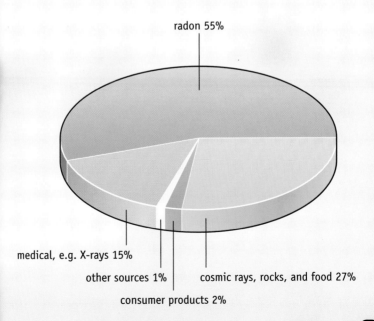

radon 55%

medical, e.g. X-rays 15%

other sources 1%

consumer products 2%

cosmic rays, rocks, and food 27%

More About Radon

Radon in homes

Materials such as rocks, soil, concrete, and brick naturally contain tiny amounts of uranium, so they may produce some radon gas. Granite is a rock that often produces radon gas, but it is not the only rock that does this, and some types of granite may not produce very much radon at all. Radon can get into houses through cracks in the walls and floors. Since it is the **densest** known gas, radon can build up to high levels in enclosed areas such as basements. In areas at risk from radon in larger amounts than usual, public authorities will take steps to advise people about the dangers of radon in the home.

There is a certain "action level" at which steps must be taken to reduce radon levels, thereby reducing the risk that it will cause lung cancer. The action involves improvements to affected homes, such as installing a "radon sump." This is a container below the house that traps the radon. Ventilation fans safely remove the radon from the sump to the outside, where it escapes harmlessly into the atmosphere.

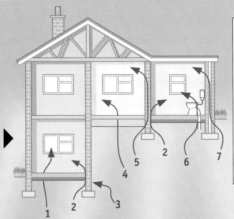

This diagram shows the different ways that radon gas can get into a building.

Where radon gets in

1 cracks in solid floors
2 construction joints
3 cracks in walls below ground level
4 gaps in suspended floors
5 cracks in walls
6 gaps around service pipes
7 cavities in walls

In the United Kingdom, the action level for radon is per 1.3 yd³ (200 Bq per m³) of air. The becquerel, Bq (pronounced 'beckerell') is the unit for measuring radioactivity, and 1 Bq is equal to one radioactive **decay** per second.

Radon daughters

When radon decays, it produces other **elements,** such as polonium, lead, and bismuth. These elements are called **radon daughters** because they come from radon. Radon daughters are very **radioactive** themselves, and are solids, not gases. They can become implanted in the lungs of anyone who breathes them in, adding to the dose of dangerous radiation. Radon and radon daughters are a problem in mines, especially uranium mines, and a lot of ventilation is needed to reduce the doses for the miners.

▼ *Radon decays to produce radon daughters along this decay chain. The big jumps are caused when the **nucleus** decays by **alpha radiation,** and the small jumps are caused when the nucleus decays by **beta radiation.** The last **isotope,** lead-206, is stable and does not decay.*

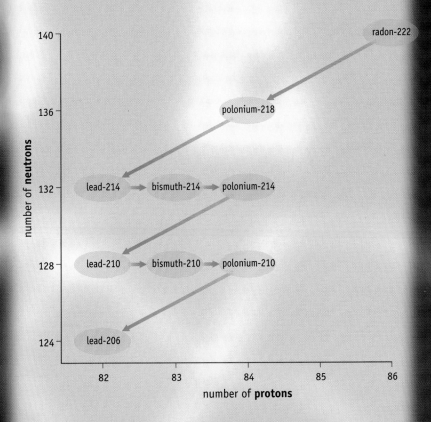

Find Out More About the Noble Gases

Elements

The table below contains some information about the properties of the noble gases.

Element	Symbol	Atomic number	Melting point °F/°C	Boiling point °F/°C	Density at 77 °/25 °C lb/ft³/kg/m³
helium	He	2	−272.2/−457.96	−268.9/−452.02	0.010/0.164
neon	Ne	10	−248.6/−415.48	−246.1/−410.98	0.052/0.825
argon	Ar	18	−189.3/−308.74	−186.0/−302.8	0.102/1.633
krypton	Kr	36	−157.2/−250.96	−153.4/−244.12	0.214/3.425
xenon	Xe	54	−111.9/−169.42	−108.1/−162.58	0.335/5.367
radon	Rn	86	−71.0/−95.8	−61.8/−79.24	0.567/9.075

Emission spectra

All the **elements** of **group** 18 are gases, so each one has a unique emission **spectrum**. This is a very useful tool for scientists who want to analyze mixtures of gases. They can detect the gases present by looking at the emission spectra.

Helium

Neon

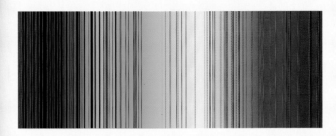

Argon

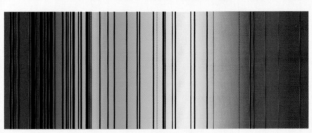

Krypton

Xenon

Radon

Find Out More (continued)

Isotopes

Although the **elements** are unreactive and do not usually form stable **compounds,** they do form **isotopes.** Isotopes of an element have identical numbers of **protons** and **electrons** but a different number of **neutrons.** The abundance is a measure of how much one isotope occurs more than another.

Helium

natural isotope	abundance (%)
^{4}He	99.99986
^{3}He	0.00014

Neon

natural isotope	abundance (%)
^{20}Ne	90.5
^{22}Ne	9.2
^{21}Ne	0.3

Argon

natural isotope	abundance (%)
^{40}Ar	99.60
^{36}Ar	0.34
^{38}Ar	0.06

natural isotope	abundance (%)
^{84}Kr	57.00
^{86}Kr	17.30
^{82}Kr	11.58
^{83}Kr	11.49
^{80}Kr	2.28
^{78}Kr	0.35

Krypton

natural isotope	abundance (%)
^{132}Xe	26.9
^{129}Xe	26.4
^{131}Xe	21.2
^{134}Xe	10.4
^{136}Xe	8.9
^{130}Xe	4.1
^{128}Xe	1.9
^{124}Xe	0.1
^{126}Xe	0.1

Xenon

isotope	half-life	
$^{222}_{86}$Rn	3.82 days	radon from radium
$^{220}_{86}$Rn	55.6 seconds	thoron from thorium
$^{219}_{86}$Rn	3.96 seconds	actinon from actinium

Radon

Glossary

absolute zero lowest temperature possible, −273.15 °C (−459.67 °F)

activated carbon type of spongelike carbon that collects molecules of other substances on its surface

alkali liquid with a pH above 7. When a base dissolves in water, it makes an alkaline solution.

alpha radiation (α radiation) waves of energy caused by quickly moving helium nuclei that have broken away from an unstable nucleus

anesthetic chemical used to numb parts of the body or to cause a patient to become unconscious in preparation for an operation

atom smallest particle of an element that has the properties of that element

atomic mass the mass of an atom

atomic number number of protons in the nucleus of an atom

background radiation small amounts of radiation from a variety of sources

beta radiation (β radiation) waves of energy consisting of fast-moving electrons produced by an unstable nucleus when it breaks up

bond force that joins atoms together

combustion chemical reaction that produces heat by a fuel reacting with oxygen in the air

compound substance made from the atoms of two or more elements, joined together by chemical bonds

condense turn from a gas into a liquid

covalent bond bond between two nonmetal atoms, made from a shared pair of electrons

decay process in which the nucleus of a radioactive substance breaks up, giving off radiation and becoming the nucleus of another element

density mass of a substance compared to its volume (how much space it takes up). To find the density or a substance, you divide its mass by its volume. Substances with a high density feel very heavy for their size.

electron particle in an atom that has a negative electric charge. Electrons are found in shells around the nucleus of an atom.

element substance made from only one type of atom

extract to remove a chemical from a mixture of chemicals

flammable able to be set on fire

fossil fuel fuel made from the ancient remains of dead animals or plants. Coal, oil, and natural gas are fossil fuels.

fractional distillation type of distillation that is used to separate mixtures of two or more liquids. It works because different liquids have different boiling points.

frequency number of waves of light per second

gamma radiation (γ radiation) powerful waves of energy caused by very high frequency light waves. Gamma radiation cannot be seen, and it can pass through metal.

group vertical column of elements in the periodic table. Elements in a group have similar properties.

half-life time taken for half the atoms of a radioactive substance to decay

inert very unreactive

infrared invisible light produced by hot objects that we can feel t as heat

ion charged particle made when atoms lose or gain electrons. If an atom loses electrons, it becomes a positive ion. If an atom gains electrons, it becomes a negative ion.

isotope atoms of an element with the same number of protons and electrons, but a different number of neutrons. Isotopes share the same atomic number but they have a different mass number.

laser stands for Light Amplification by Stimulated Emission of Radiation. Laser light has special properties, including a small range of frequencies and very little spreading out.

liquefy turn a gas into a liquid by cooling it or putting it under pressure

mass number the number of protons added to the number of neutrons in an atom's nucleus

mass spectrometer machine that analyzes a tiny amount of a substance and detects the different chemicals it contains

mineral substance that is found naturally in the earth but does not come from animals or plants. Metal ores and limestone are minerals.

molecule smallest particle of an element or compound that exists by itself. A molecule is made from two or more atoms joined together.

neutron particle in an atom's nucleus that does not have an electric charge

nonrenewable not able to be replaced once it has run out

nucleus center part of an atom made from protons and neutrons that has a positive electric charge

ore substance containing minerals from which metals can be taken out and purified

oxidizing agent chemical that can oxidize other chemicals by adding oxygen to them or removing electrons from them. It is also called an oxidant.

period horizontal row of elements in the periodic table

periodic table chart in which all the known elements are arranged into groups and periods

phosphor chemical that gives off light when it absorbs energy

pitch highness or lowness of a sound

prism block of transparent material, usually glass, that has a triangular cross-section

proton particle in a atom's nucleus that has a positive electric charge

radiation energy or particles given off when an atom decays

radioactive producing radiation

radiosonde package of scientific equipment carried into the air by a balloon

radon daughter radioactive element produced when radon decays. Also called radon progeny, these include lead, polonium, and bismuth.

reaction chemical change that produces new substances

refining removing impurities from a substance to make it more pure. It can also mean separating the different substances in a mixture, for example, in oil refining.

semiconductor substance, such as silicon, that is an electrical insulator at room temperature, but a conductor when it is warmed or other elements are added to it

solar eclipse event in which the Moon is exactly between the Sun and Earth, blocking the Sun's energy from reaching parts of Earth

spectroscope piece of equipment that splits the light given off by something into its spectrum

spectrum all the different colors that make up a ray of light

subatomic particle particle smaller than an atom, such as a proton, neutron, or electron

superconductor substance that has no electrical resistance. Most superconductors need to be kept very cold.

transformer electrical device that converts low-voltage electricity to a higher voltage, or high-voltage electricity into a lower voltage

ultraviolet invisible light just beyond the blue end of the spectrum

viscosity measure of how easily something flows from place to place. A substance with a low viscosity is very runny.

welding joining two or more metals together, usually by heating them

Timeline

helium discovered in the Sun	1868	Pierre Janssen
helium isolated	1895	William Ramsay
neon isolated	May 1898	William Ramsay and Morris Travers
krypton isolated	June 1898	William Ramsay and Morris Travers
xenon isolated	July 1898	William Ramsay and Morris Travers
radon discovered	1900	Friedrich Dorn
radon isolated	1910	William Ramsay and Robert Whytlaw-Gray

Further Reading and Useful Websites

Books

Fullick, Ann. *Science Topics: Chemicals in Action*. Chicago: Heinemann Library, 1999.

Oxlade, Chris. *Chemicals in Action* series, *Elements and Compounds* and *States of Matter*. Chicago: Heinemann Library, 2002.

Snedden, Robert. *Material World: Solids, Liquids and Gases*. Chicago: Heinemann 2001.

Websites

1001 Periodic Table Quiz Questions
http://www.1001-periodic-table-quiz-questions.com
Hundreds of multiple choice questions to test your knowledge.

Creative Chemistry
http://www.creative-chemistry.org.uk
An interactive chemistry site with fun practical activities, quizzes, puzzles, and more.

DiscoverySchool
http://school.discovery.com/students
Help for science projects and homework, and free science clip art.

Mineralogy Database
http://www.webmineral.com
Lots of useful information about minerals, including color photographs and information about their chemistry.

Proton Don
http://www.funbrain.com/periodic
The fun periodic table quiz!

WebElements™
http://www.webelements.com
An interactive periodic table crammed with information and photographs.

Index

ML

2/04